Walking Throug

Sharing my personal experiences of
Apparitions, Locutions and Healings
in Medjugorje
since my first pilgrimage in 1986

Alison Riggott

Foreword

I was encouraged to write

Walking Through The Vines –
my Medjugorje testimony

after reading in the Mass Readings for the day:

"Do not forget the things your eyes have seen, nor let them slip from your heart all the days of your life; rather tell them to your children and to your children's children" (Deut 4:1. 5-9)

So with thanks to Mary and Her Son Jesus I share these wonderful experiences with my family, my friends, and with you, so that you may experience in some way the joy of walking with Mary –

I have been visiting Medjugorje for over twenty three years now, spending over a hundred days there, usually with a group of pilgrims, and more recently I have travelled independently and spent two months in healing prayer for other pilgrims.

The messages have not changed since Our Lady first appeared to six young people in 1981. Mary continues to call us to pray, to fast and confess, to love, to be peace-makers, to ongoing conversion and to have hope. She said through Ivan
"If you are strong in hope, the church has hope"

The messages are constant and have not changed but I have most certainly changed.
Each time I go I am at a different stage in my conversion and I receive exactly what I need to help me move on to the next stage of my faith journey.

Introduction

In September 1986 I was at a Justice & Peace meeting when someone mentioned that Our Lady was appearing to six young people in Yugoslavia and calling herself the Queen of Peace.
I was fascinated by this and tried to find out more.
My brother in law, Pete, found an article written by Wayne Weible recording all the facts.

When I read that Mary had been appearing every day in this Communist country for five years I had very mixed emotions – very similar to when I first read about the Baptism in the Holy Spirit.
I was determined to go – despite having four young sons aged six to twelve – but I also felt angry that my church was not telling us that the mother of our Saviour was taking the trouble to appear daily on earth with messages for us all.
Our church hierarchy is very pharisaic most of the time.
I felt nothing short of a compulsion to go and found a small travel company arranging trips from Heathrow to stay with local families.
There were no guest houses or hotels in those days.
I asked a couple of friends to join me and my husband agreed to look after the boys with family help.
I saved my earnings from my work as a carer in a residential home, filled the fridge, and flew out in November for five days.
The flight was exciting in itself because I hadn't been on a plane since I was eleven when I went to Lourdes with my primary school. I was now thirty three.
We flew to Split which was quite hostile and boarded a coach, crossing two borders where our passports were closely scrutinised, and arrived in Medjugorje in the early hours of the morning.

Early Days 1986 Miracles and Visions

When I got off the bus in Medjugorje I was struck by the crescent moon and a single star, which I sensed was very significant. It reminded me of Mary nursing the child Jesus.

Five days later we left in the middle of the night and there was a full moon, which accompanied us to the airport. I sat alone watching this moon and praying because I could see the face of Mary in the moon. After a while the image changed to that of a boy's face, but the features remained the same. I thought it must be the face of the child Jesus.

When we arrived at Split airport, my friend Elaine asked me if I had seen the moon. Her expression told me that she too had been struck by its appearance. I told her what I had seen and she had also seen the face of Mary, but added that

"It seemed to change to a child's face"

About a month later I was asked to share my experience of Medjugorje with an ecumenical youth group.

 I was a bit nervous about it as I set out but as I got into my car I looked up – and there was a full moon with a face of the child Jesus again, as if to give me reassurance.

I have not seen this since!.

Early Days 1986 Miracles and Visions

We were welcomed by our host with smiles and hugs – she spoke no English.

After a bowl of hot soup Elaine and I were shown to our bedroom – a converted barn up a rickety stairwell. I woke at dawn to an unfamiliar sound and looking out of the window saw the pigs beneath us.

Our host was throwing food to them with one hand, and holding a rosary in the other. Welcome to Medjugorje!

Each morning I awoke to the sight of her, dressed in black, feeding the pigs and chickens outside my window, with her rosary beads in hand.

Early Days 1986 Miracles and Visions

She fed her five visitors well, always offering seconds and home-made wine, but we stopped having a second helping when we realised that her sons had the left-overs from our meal.

There were no toilets at this time – just a shed with holes in the ground, and the route to the church was through the vineyards

Praying with The Visionaries

Because of the travelling time I only had three days in Medjugorje. There was a daily Mass in the evening following the rosary, and further prayers afterwards, lasting three hours altogether – all in Croatian.

Yet the locals filled the church every evening after a day's work and I was particularly struck by the number of young men fervently praying.

Every evening the visionaries had an apparition in the priest's house before Mass began and we were fortunate to meet with Vicksta, Ivan and Fr Joso.

On the last day we gathered outside the priest's house for the time of apparition, armed with rosary beads and medals to take home. We were about fifty yards away from the house, behind a big crowd of Italians, when suddenly a Franciscan pointed to Elaine and I and beckoned us in.

We were so surprised but the crowd seemed to part as we walked forward and the next minute we were kneeling next to Jacov and Maria as they began to pray the rosary.

Suddenly, they stopped and their eyes looked up to the wall and they were both in animated conversation with Our Lady.

After a few minutes, Maria continued to finish the rosary and, through an interpreter, told us that Our Lady sees us all and blesses us all and our families, and all the holy objects we are carrying (we were laden!)

That must be one of the most surreal moments of my life.

The Voice of God

I have heard 'the voice of God' six times in my life to date, four of these in Medjugorje. Once I was on Podboro hill, late in the afternoon on the last day of a pilgrimage. I had taken a group of about ten people and we had climbed Podboro together.

They all returned to the church in time for the apparition and Mass but I stayed awhile alone.

I was sitting on a rock and telling God that of course it was a privilege to bring people here, and they had had a very fruitful time, but I had been so busy caring for them that I hadn't got as much out of the pilgrimage as usual. I was having a bit of a moan really. Immediately, a voice of authority in my head clearly said

"Some people need consoling and some are consolers. Will you be one of my consolers?"

I was quite shaken and totally transformed. "Yes Lord, of course I will!" All tiredness and self-pity left. I skipped down the hill and sat on a bench outside the church. Mass had begun.

A young man in his twenties with a London accent sat next to me and asked if he could talk to me. He told me that he had been here a week and was returning tomorrow but he was still tormented because he had persuaded his girlfriend to have an abortion against her will and he could not forgive himself.

I told him to go and receive communion and offer it up for his unborn child, to pray that his child is received in the Kingdom, and to name his child as he receives Jesus.

Off he went. I was delighted that he came to find me after Mass. "Justin!" he said.

He told me that as he received communion, the name Justin filled his head. He looked so happy.

A White Orchid

I came out of confession with a priest who had just been reconciled himself, and saw the sun spinning as white as a Host, then met Maria, an elderly polish lady who was taken from her home when she was sixteen because she would not sign a paper to renounce her faith. She was beaten, taken to Siberia and lived in a concentration camp for three years. She and her mother and sister lived on a cup of flour mixed with water each day. The guards would ask "Why are you still alive?" and she would reply "God keeps me alive" For one week she had no water. She saw Jesus many times and now prays for others in hospital and at home.

I walked in the woodland with Maria and we prayed together. She told me she felt such joy when she touched me that she knew God had great joy to give me.

"Jesus is going to open a door into a beautiful garden and you will have such joy"

We talked of many things and then saw a white orchid at our feet which had not been there when we sat down.
It seemed to be a gift to us from Gospa.
Maria went back the next day to show someone else the orchid but it was not there. I also have visited on my own. Once I saw it but it was not there the next day.

Twelve years later I visited an old friend (who had anonymously sponsored my son Ben on a trip to Medjugorje when he was thirteen) and she showed me a photograph of a white orchid.

She told me that she and a few friends had been really taken by a white flower which had burst through the rocky soil on Podboro and one of the friends took a photograph of it for her.

A White Orchid

This was on the 25th of April 1989 – the day of the monthly message from Our Lady – and they were finding it difficult to hear the message.
Later they were told the message in full which included the words,

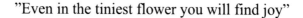

"Even in the tiniest flower you will find joy"

As I stood in Vicksta's garden I was nearly crushed between the Spanish and Italians – an unpleasant experience but I thought of the crowds desperate to see Jesus and imagined the stretcher being lowered through the roof.
Also understood the anger of the authority 'in control' and why they wanted to be rid of Him.

Our Lady of Medjugorje

I first saw this picture in 1997 when I went to Sheila Cronin's house to arrange my next trip to Medjugorje. Sheila had taken a picture the year before at the time of Apparition on Podboro Hill.

She had taken a picture of the tree with the sunset behind it.

When the photos were developed this image of Our Lady holding rosary beads came out. Sheila gave me a copy and I have used it for contemplation since then.

For several years I could see the outline of Our Lady behind the tree, I have always been taken with the size of her hands – big enough to hold all our prayers.

Then, after a few years I was able to see another face behind her – I contemplate on this as God the Father. Sometimes I see the Holy Spirit in the form of a dove across the centre.

However, the most recent change in what I see really took my breath away.

In 2005 Patrick Lynch and I formed the Healing Light Ministry following a pilgrimage to Medjugorje. At Easter 2006 we shared in the passion and crucifixion of Jesus for the first time. Since then, Patrick has shared a mystical crucifixion every Friday. He often feels the five wounds of Jesus including the Crown of Thorns.

One evening I was in my bedroom getting ready for bed when I glanced at the picture and all I could see was the bleeding face of Jesus with a crown of thorns on His head.

I now see this every time I look at the picture… I see this image in the centre of the photo, in Mary's heart.

Mary always points us to Her Son………

Our Lady of Medjugorje

The Journey Continues

In 1997 I was climbing Krusevec in my bare feet as I have done on every visit before without much difficulty. However, I found it incredibly difficult and was straggling behind the others.

After the fourth station where Mary meets Jesus, the pain was intense.
I had a glimpse of His suffering and tried to offer it up but each step brought such pain and took my breath away. Then I simply could not move – could not put one foot in front of another. I was prevented from moving.
I sat down on a stone and listened to Jesus.

"I choose your path in life, for some I choose a path of suffering because in the suffering they find Me.
But for you I choose joy. Not all can find Me in joy."

I put my shoes back on and caught up with the others, feeling quite humbled but delighted to be a child of joy.
We do not choose our path or circumstances.
Just as I cannot learn through suffering as Patrick can – I can learn of His love and joy through other gifts.
It is not possible for some to see Him in a material, western world or in the spiritual hunger of others.

But I see Jesus in the eyes of His chosen ones,
I smell the perfume of His mother Mary
I am a consoler, by the grace of God.

The Journey Continues

In 2003 I went in thanksgiving for twenty five years since I was baptised in the Spirit. The visit was a fiftieth birthday present from my son Chris. May he and his brothers be blessed for bringing their mother to the Mother of God.

I climbed Podboro alone and in a group. I climbed Krusevec twice in one day.

I wiped a tear from the statue of the Risen Lord, and received overwhelming grace as I reflected on that momentous day twenty five years previously when I received the gift of

Baptism in The Holy Spirit

At the age of twenty five I had the most wonderful infilling of the Holy Spirit, whilst peeling potatoes, which exposed my soul and enriched my life beyond compare. On a Tuesday afternoon in May, 1978 whilst my four and three year olds were watching Playschool, and month old baby Ben was asleep, Chris was not yet born, I was peeling the potatoes at my kitchen sink looking out of the window and talked to God. I thanked Him for sending His son Jesus to us, and acknowledged that Jesus had died on a Cross to take away our sins... and asked Him to fill me with His Holy Spirit..... and He did.

I began to pray out loud the prayer that Jesus had taught us whilst on earth, the Our Father, and suddenly I realised that I was not praying in English but in a strange language. The whole kitchen took on an ethereal golden light and I was totally full of Joy – I thought I would explode. This Joy has remained within me for over thirty years now. It is like a stream within me; sometimes it goes underground awhile but then re-emerges bubbling noisily and spilling out over the edges of its bank to refresh those around me. It is a stream that nourishes and sustains, that cleanses and reassures, that removes doubt.

It is full of mercy and healing power and love.

I entered this stream of the Holy Spirit and got very involved in Catholic Charismatic Renewal, leading prayer groups, organising speakers and retreats, regular Renewal Masses and became a diocesan coordinator for CCR.

The Scent of Roses

On Monday 2nd June 2003 I was privileged to be present at two apparitions. Miryana has an apparition on the 2nd of each month and pilgrims are invited to be present. This is usually a personal message for Miryana. What a privilege to see the ecstasy on her face as she gazes up at Our Lady – and what sadness fills her when it comes to an end. As she passed through the crowd to return home, I could smell roses. It reminded me of a time before when I stood in Ivan's garden listening to him and then I could smell the sweetest rose. I looked all around the garden to find its source but in vain. Later I was told the smell of roses is often associated with the presence of Our Lady.

On returning home, I was surrounded by the scent once again as I re-read the words of Mary given to us by Ivan:
"I have come because I have been sent by my Son to help you"
Ivan is the eldest of the visionaries, now married with children. He has grown in patience, confidence and wisdom since I first saw him. He says that Our Lady does not get bored with giving messages to the world and he has learnt the importance of this from her.
He never gets bored from telling pilgrims repeatedly, through interpreters, the messages of Mary.

Pilgrim People

Podboro is the hill where the apparitions first took place in 1981 and is quite unspoilt, with a statue of Our Lady and the Crucified Christ on the site of the early apparitions

The climb to the top of the hill is marked by beautiful Italian plaques depicting the Joyful mysteries of the rosary.

It's good to go up alone or with a small group of friends but I am always surprised by what I receive and learn when climbing with a large group.

During one climb I was overwhelmed by the struggle around me – the symbolic journey of pilgrim people on their struggle to reach the mountain top of God.

I felt such love for these people and Jesus seemed to say:

"What you feel is a glimpse of My love for you. Now do you understand why I died for you on Calvary?"

All ages, all physical conditions struggling up in the heat, helping each other along – an elderly lady (usually in a wheelchair) walked up with help and inspired an arthritic lady to follow her, just one

Pilgrim People

glowing example of how we can all inspire each other to do the impossible.

A pilgrim people like any other group of pilgrims travelling over the centuries.

It reminds me of the Israelites on their way to the Promised Land, of people seeking asylum, of groups travelling to Jerusalem or Mecca or shrines throughout the world.

It is the epitome of our church as we walk alongside each other in our daily struggle.

Sometimes I lead the group, choosing the path for others to follow, then I'll slip back to be in the body of the group, close to the heart.

But most of all I like to be at the back because it reminds me of the Holy Spirit, urging, encouraging, comforting His people.

One day I climbed Podboro full of joy and thanks. I passed a noisy Italian group at the Annunciation plaque and stopped at the first cross where Mary appeared in the early days.

I was fascinated by an army of ants travelling from their ant hole about ten metres to a pile of husks from dead grasses – all processing along and then the worker ants collecting a single husk and carrying it back.

Some came back empty handed, some laboured with different size husks. Most went head first into the ant hole, husk first. One ant was carrying a huge husk, larger than average.

I thought 'that's Patrick' swimming against the tide, a heavy cross, stopping to pick it up whenever he dropped it.

This ant had a problem getting past a twig but he persevered and crossed it. I stayed to watch how he would get it into the hole.

Impossible head first because the husk was too big so he circled the hole a few times, took hold of the husk and slid in backwards pulling it with him.

Perseverance, endurance and brains – never mind stubborn-ness.

Pilgrim People

Then I climbed the hill, sat on a rock and looked down at the valley, and there was a procession of people making their way on the paths through the grapevines – some to Podboro, some to Krusevec, some to church.

They looked just like the ants and I wondered how many would return home empty handed, how many would not persevere with the grain given them.

I thought of the procession in church as we go to Communion, how many go up empty handed, and how many return full of the love and mercy of Jesus in their very being. I weep at the thought of others who receive the Lord and don't give him another thought, yet carry Him within them.

As I came down the hill I met a man giving witness.

He had been away from the church for forty years.

When his wife died, a young neighbour who went to the local catholic church told him about Medjugorje.

He wasn't interested but she gave him a leaflet about a trip and he thought he might as well go.

At first he felt out of his depth and out of place but Mary's miracle worked and before the end of the week he received the Sacraments of Reconciliation and Eucharist and started going to church again when he returned home.

More importantly, he was at peace with himself and with God.

Pilgrim People

Krusevec, or Cross mountain is more of a challenge. It is a place of historic significance for the country and where atrocities have taken place in previous centuries.

In 1933 local villagers carried the huge white stones to the summit to build a cross marking nineteen hundred years of Christianity. This was under the direction of the parish priest. Twenty years later another priest decided to build the white, twin-towered church of St James in Medjugorje – far too big for it's time – but now every seat is filled and there are another four thousand seats outside. Krusevec now has plaques depicting the stations of the Cross to help the pilgrims focus on the passion, death and resurrection of Jesus. We follow the way of the Cross with Our Lady, and see her son's horrific journey through her eyes and begin to understand the immensity of His love for us.

One image which remains with me is the sight of five young men in their twenties carrying a paralysed man down the mountain on a stretcher.
Somehow they had carried him all the way up to the Cross and down again – out of love and faith and hope.
God bless them each time this image is recalled.

Pilgrim People

From the top of Krusevec you can look down on Medjugorje and the other two hamlets with the church in the centre. Of course it has spread out over the last twenty years to cater for over thirty million pilgrims but the essence remains the same and the enlargement has been sensitively carried out. Now Medjugorje has many guest houses, hotels and restaurants, out of necessity but I treasure those memories before even a café was built.

Mary has told the visionaries that she chose this place because of the strong faith upheld there. For four hundred years the Franciscans held the faith despite invasions and Communist rule. Our Lady first appeared on June 24th 1981, the feast of John the Baptist, exactly ten years before war broke out.

Her messages have not changed because like a good mother repeatedly telling her child not to touch a hot fire or to run across a road, so Mary continues to chide us, protect us, warn us and encourage us. Mary is Mother to all. Once, a visionary asked her about prayer and Mary told her that a Muslim lady in the village gives the best example of how to pray – because she prays with her heart.

Fireworks, Golden Rosaries and A Nun's Conversion!

My friends were sharing a house with a reluctant pilgrim whom I shall call Sister Marian.

During the first meal on our arrival she told us that she did not really want to be there... a nun in her community had been many times and was always talking about Medjugorje, eventually wearing her resistance down until she agreed to visit with another sister from their community.

Unfortunately her friend was ill and unable to travel so she was here on her own – and already regretting it!!

We took her under our wing and befriended her for the week.

On the last evening of the pilgrimage Ivan invited pilgrims to be present at the Blue Cross while he had an apparition.

.

We wrapped up and walked to the site of the Blue cross which was already very crowded.

We found a few rocks in close proximity so I left my friends and Sr Marian there, and climbed up higher myself where there was more room.

During the apparition I saw a beam of light and felt tremendous peace and joy, and felt so privileged to be there.

Afterwards I walked back to the house and found my friends.

Fireworks, Golden Rosaries and A Nun's Conversion!

They were on such a high and said "Wasn't that amazing!"
I could see they had experienced something very special so asked them to tell me what they had seen.
Alex told me that as they sat on the rocks during the apparition they saw beams of coloured light, darting about.
This intensified as if it was a firework display, and the beams of light were surrounding them.
One of my friends and Sr Marian were actually frightened and suggested they should move but they were reassured that this was a sign for them – to confirm that the apparition was taking place.
People around them started to leave as the apparition reached its conclusion but they were transfixed to the spot because of the 'firework' display going on all around them. Eventually it ended and they came away incredulous that no-one else had seen it.

The next morning we boarded the coach to leave, and the difference in Sr Marian was astounding.
Her faith had been rekindled and she was laughing like a child. She couldn't wait to see her community sister and tell her that the message of Medjugorje was real!
Praise and Thank You Jesus and Mary.
It is not uncommon for Rosary beads to turn to gold in Medjugorje.
My friends and I also were graced by Rosaries and Crucifixes turning in this way.
Anne, one of my friends felt the Rosary hot in her hands as she prayed – imagine how she felt when she saw it had turned gold..
The Rosary I had borrowed from my Grandad for my first visit turned to gold in my suitcase – I didn't own one in those Charismatic days!
A sceptical priest came to look at it and having seen he believed!
"It is gold"

Healing Light Ministry

During a week's pilgrimage in 2005, the seeds were sown to form the Healing Light Ministry which has since developed into a full time ministry of healing, prayer and evangelisation

Healing Light Ministry

"Come to Medjugorje heal my people"

In September 2006 I returned for a month with Patrick.
We went on blind faith, following three 'internal' calls *"Come to Medjugorje, heal my people"*. We wondered how people with different languages would understand us but were given to understand that this would not be a problem, and it wasn't!
We arrived on Wednesday and that evening we went to outdoor Adoration.

"Before you loved God, He loved you first"

A full moon in a clear sky had the face of Jesus.

Welcome back to Medjugorje!

Healing Light Ministry

Each day during our pilgrimage we prayed the Divine Office and joined other pilgrims at Mass, Adoration and the Rosary

Many healings took place; the majority of them in the area around the Statue of The Risen Lord.

The statue of the Risen Lord is beautiful and water drips in droplets from the right knee, which is above head height.

It is unexplained, but now scientifically found to be the consistency of tears.

In 2003 I was praying near the Cross and mindful of a woman sobbing just in front of me.

I started to pray silently for her and was given to understand that it was Mary's tears as she stood at the foot of the Cross which are pouring out.

I went to tell the woman that she is not alone, but standing and weeping with Mary.

Three years later I read that a man prayed for an explanation and he also understood that they were Mary's tears as she stood at the foot of the cross.

We prayed for a woman who had been missing for four days and later that evening we heard she had been found alive on Cross mountain, dehydrated but OK. Praise Jesus.

Healing Light Ministry

We spoke to a woman with heavily bandaged legs, who had suffered for some time. She asked us not to pray for her healing 'in case He sent her something worse'. She then made the sign of the cross on our foreheads with the tissue, saying God bless you, and walked away.

A lady from America was "told" she would meet us to pray for healing her grief. Her son had been killed in an accident on a building site. We walked with her from the statue to Fr Slavko's tomb and entrusted Christopher (her son) to Fr Slavko – there was a rose glistening on the tomb, she gasped when she saw it and said "that's the rose that was on my bed when I woke this morning"! Great healing was taking place.
When she realised her son was safe with Mary she was all peaceful and smiling and full of thanks.
"I will pray for you as long as I live" "May you live forever" replied Patrick.

We prayed silently, for a couple at the Risen Lord statue.
They looked dreadful, didn't want to be together, miserable, she walked with a limp.
We took on a lot of their emotional pain which we had to pray for well into the night.
Two days later we were delighted to see them walking arm in arm laughing and chatting on their way together for a meal. Praise God.

A woman came to us who had been 'told' the night before she would see someone healing who she should approach and ask for prayer for her bad back; her husband pointed us out.
She told us she had chronic back pain for years and nothing she did seemed to ease it. She had come to Medjugorje in great hope.
We prayed together for a while and Patrick felt the pain.
When we saw her again that evening she was walking with her husband, pain free.

The Gifts of Healing and Languages (Tongues)

One evening as we walked towards the Risen Lord statue, praying the rosary, I saw a woman lying unconscious on the grass surrounded by four people. She was very white. I continued praying the rosary while Patrick knelt down beside her. We said two more Hail Marys to the end of the decade, then I prayed in tongues. Patrick placed his hand on her forehead and said "Come back to us".

Immediately her eyes opened, she smiled, put her hands together in prayer and touched his cheeks saying, "Gratis", then sat up.

A man asked me if I was German. I said "No, I'm English" He said "But you speak German?" I said "No, I only speak English." He replied "But you were speaking German!"

In the meantime the people surrounding the recovered lady were speaking Italian and Spanish to Patrick. She had fully recovered, was fine and able to get up, so we walked on.

While we continued our walk towards the cemetery a voice from the shadows called out "Excuse me, do you speak English?" We turned round to see him. He said "I am Bosnia, my name is Dominic. I have been coming here for five days and I have nothing. I have been to the priests and they won't give me anything, they say I need a letter from my priest"

At first I thought he meant he was getting nothing spiritual out of the place, then realised he had no money. He said he had been sleeping under the vines. I told Patrick and we gave him all our coins – only about six euros. We turned to leave but Patrick said he would say a prayer. He put his hand on Dominic's shoulder and prayed in another language very slowly and deliberately. Dominic understood him. Three times he looked up, each time more amazed. Patrick blessed him on the forehead and we said "God Bless" Dominic shook our hands and said "Thank you and Good luck"

We turned to leave and he put his head in his hands and wept.

We walked away and I was quite overcome with a sense of being in the presence of God. I cried out with joy.

The Gifts of Healing and Languages (Tongues)

Then we sat down near the Transfiguration plaque to pray. Dominic strode past into town, smiled again and said "Thank you again and God Bless".

He walked with great purpose and a strong stride.

We were given to understand that Patrick had told him where to get bread, where to go for shelter and where to find work in the fields, later still we learned Patrick had spoken to him in a Serbo/Croat dialect.

We continued praying and passed a woman, sitting alone.

She asked if we knew where the grave yard was so we asked if she wanted to walk with us. We invited her to join us in the rosary as we walked.

We went into the graveyard and prayed for a while at Fr Slavko's grave and got up to leave.

I rejoice with you and I desire to tell you that your brother Slavko has been born into heaven and intercedes for you.
part message, November 25, 2000

She walked out with us and said she had sat there for two nights, not having the courage to go in alone.

This was her last night and she had asked Our Lady to send her someone to take her in.

She had travelled from Dublin and wanted to pray at Fr Slavko's grave for her deceased parents before she left. She was so grateful and prayerful for having met us.

Gate and Hidden Stream (Grace)

During prayer a gate at Mortehoe in Devon came to mind. As you approach the gate, you can hear a stream before you can see it

Dear God, so often I can hear the stream of grace before I can see it.
I have learnt to recognise the sound of the stream and follow it,
knowing its reality will become clearer once it is followed.
Jesus, you are human yet divine.
You sit astride the gate with one foot on earth, the other in heaven.
And yet You are the Gate, the only Way, Truth and Life.
You bring your divinity into our humanity, not only by becoming one
of us, but especially in the Eucharist.
We offer ourselves, our humanity of weaknesses and faults and You
change us.
You transform us into something divine.
Sometimes we are in one place and would like to be in another but
can't move.
We don't have to.
We invite Your light into our darkness to change us, to illuminate us
and heal us.
To transform us.

I ponder on the Mysteries of Light:
At Your baptism You changed the relationship between God and
mankind and our wholeness began.

You changed water into wine.

At transfiguration your whole being became light.

At the Passover meal you changed bread and wine into your own
Body and Blood.

So it is not surprising that we too can be so utterly changed!

Kravica Waterfall

We got a taxi to the waterfall at Kravica – absolutely staggering! We stood at the top near a deep, still pool and saw the reflection of the sun in the water, spinning, dancing, like a host, surrounded by blue and red.

The clouds were reflected on either side.

It was like looking into the vault of heaven, an aperture leading to a place of pure light.

Then it was like looking into my own soul, a beautiful place, bigger than I could have imagined and full of opportunity and adventure.

I used to think my soul was inside my body but now I know my body is inside my soul, which lights up in prayer.

Then to the waterfall.

Immense power as water plunges over the cliff on three sides of the river and pours out of the cliff face itself.

A never-ending flow, even in this dry season, of pure, cleansing, refreshing, healing, living water.

We swam in the cold water of the river feeling refreshed in Body Mind and Spirit

Like the deer that yearns for running streams
So are our souls thirsting for You O Lord.

Passion and Crucifixion

During prayer one afternoon we once again had a passion and crucifixion experience lasting three hours. Not as traumatic as last time because at least we knew what was happening – our first mystical crucifixion experience was in Ilfracombe, during Easter week, after being part of the Healing Ministry at the Celebrate Conference.

One evening, we were praying together when Patrick felt unwell. He thought he had food poisoning at first but the symptoms spread. I asked the Lord what was happening and was told

"You are standing at the foot of the cross with Mary and the other women"

I asked Patrick if he was on the Cross and he said "Yes"

He was in a lot of pain and I asked him to tell me where it hurt when he could speak. He then mentioned different parts of his body as they got worse – his feet, his ankles, his shoulders, his forehead, eyes, hands, side, and his skin felt like it was on fire.

His lips were swollen and very dry so I got him some water.

After some time each pain lessened until he said "It's done"

I said "Is it accomplished?" and he said "Yes"

Over three hours had passed although it seemed like ten minutes

After this I was given word from Ezekiel 2 to read, they were the same as this morning's office:

"to bring Truth to His church".

Then directed to read Acts 2 –

"the house was shaken on the first Pentecost."

Patrick has continued to have these mystical crucifixions every Friday since Easter 2005. They have extended and often begin on Thursday evening and last until the Saturday. They are a time of Grace and we offer them for all who ask for prayer and healing –

family, friends and people who contact us by telephone or email from all over the world.

The Holy Spirit is not constrained by Time or Space!

'There's an Apparition Tonight'

One evening while walking to Fr Slavko's grave towards Krusevec. I prayed silently for an infilling for Patrick as he had had a tough day taking emotional and physical pain from people we had been praying with.

Immediately he saw the figure of Jesus on the cross on the mountain all lit up (there are no lights on the Cross).

Later that evening, while having a meal, I said "There's an apparition tonight at the Blue Cross but it's not public knowledge".

I just heard the words in my head.

After the meal we walked to the Risen Lord statue to see who needed prayer and as we were walking home we stopped and watched a most wonderful 'fireworks' display of lightening over Podboro which lasted over five minutes.

There were about ten other people with us. I told them there was an apparition, but they didn't look very sure!

Our friend with whom we had shared an Emmaus experience the previous day confirmed there had been an apparition when we met him again the following morning.

'There's an Apparition Tonight'

He was delighted to have been at the Blue Cross for Ivan's apparition the previous night but said it had not been public knowledge because of the wet weather. He had not seen any lightening. He was leaving the next day and was still hoping for some sign before he left, although he knew he should not look for signs.

It was the time of the daily apparition and I saw the sun spinning so I told him to look at the sun.
(He had been unable to look until now because he thought, wisely, it would hurt his eyes)
But Medjugorje is a very special place, so I told him to trust and look and he did and he saw it spinning, like a host, while we prayed for him.
He left full of joy, praise and love.

The following morning we went to Croatian Mass and afterwards went for a long walk.
An American woman was sitting on the steps to our apartments when we returned.
She said she didn't feel well, was very tired, and sat down and asked the Lord to help her.
She just knew that if she waited someone would come along and be able to help her.
We told her we had a healing ministry and she took this as an answer to prayer.
She confided all her problems to us especially those involving her daughter.
We prayed for her and her daughter and off she went with a smile on her face.
I had a siesta and was woken by a dream -

"The Truth will set you free"

Discipleship and The Cross

More prayer later in the kitchen, infilling and mighty tremors.
Patrick was asked to carry the Cross.
He saw and felt the crown of thorns.
At the same time I saw Jesus' eyes in Patrick's and was 'told' that these convulsions I was witnessing were the convulsions Jesus bore whilst on the Cross as his whole nervous system collapsed.
Mary saw what I saw.
Also 'told' that the tremblings resembled the tremblings of great fear that Jesus bore in Gethsemane.

I climbed Podboro reflectively and had a deeper understanding of discipleship.
I sat under the crucifix for some time and 'saw' the blood of Jesus pouring out of his body back into the earth and poor Mary at the foot of the cross, her hands covered in blood, saw the gruesomeness of it all.
I thought about the hurry to take his body away before sunset.
The sun was dancing and winking away on the way down. I went to the Risen Lord and prayed the stations of the cross, identifying with each station as I carry my cross.
Meanwhile Patrick had climbed Krusevec to rededicate us and our ministry and had an experience of Abraham offering his son Isaac. He made a further commitment of obedience and acceptance to God's will.
We had an email to say that a friend had had C.A.T. scan and her tumour had disappeared.
We had prayed with this friend some months ago, over the telephone. She had been ill for ten years with chronic fatigue, sickness, and depression.
Today she is fully active leading Alpha and Prayer groups

Praise and Thank you Jesus.

The Face of Jesus

Lots of shakes and tremors during morning prayer.

We went to the English mass. Powerful consecration.

More shakes for Patrick who can't get up from kneeling position. I was given further understanding of discipleship (St Matthew's feast day, leave your home and family.)

Very conscious of being Soldiers for Christ and was told that by becoming disciples we share in the redemption and healing of our families.

After communion I 'saw' the eye of Jesus, closed and bruised, side profile; then both eyes and battered face.

I 'heard' God telling me gently:

"Now you know why I couldn't let you see the face of Jesus before when you asked me. It would have been too awful for you"

(In prayer, I have often asked to see His face just once!) This has been denied me until now out of love.

Patrick was quite sore and shaken after mass and had to lie down. The attack lasted until mid-day, then we walked steadily to the foot of the mountain and round to Blue Cross where apparition often takes place. Patrick asked me if the smell of roses was coming from the flowers round the statue. They were all artificial and I could not smell anything!

Then to Adoration and to Risen Lord statue. As we were leaving Patrick asked me if the face of the statue looked different tonight. It did. It was facing forward rather than sideways, eyes half closed, nose battered – awful.

Lovely prayerful morning having dreamt of people pouring out of the church clothed in red and white signifying the blood and water flowing from His side - Divine Mercy. Then saw a door and heard two knocks. The door was ajar and someone, Jesus, waiting to be invited in. Intense bright white light emanating from person behind the door – Jesus. We went to a great mass and heard a homily on Moses and the Spirit falling on the seventy two in the tent plus the two who were in the 'wrong place'

Know the feeling very well!

Miryana's Apparition

Waited from 7.30 till 9 00am leaning against the wall of the building where the apparition was to take place.

About fifteen minutes before the apparition I smelt roses and internally asked "What is this?" I was given to understand that Miryana was leaving her house to prepare for the apparition, and to be ready. Last week at her home, Miryana described how she felt before her monthly apparition. She is so excited leading up to it, she stays awake all night in prayer to be ready. She begins each day with an 'Our Father' from the heart to help her pray. As she arrived some of the huge crowd applauded – I'm sure she doesn't like it, she would prefer them to be praying. We all prayed seven Our Fathers, Hail Marys and Glory Be together, then the Resurrection mystery, then sudden silence. Everyone was looking west towards the door of the building but we looked east towards the sun. I saw a golden monstrance with rays of golden grace pouring from it. Then it became a red heart. I felt overwhelmed with the love of Jesus. After a while we were given a draft translation of the message – *"I love you into eternity. Many of you have faith but not love. You must love one another and grow in love of God."* Then Miryana shared a personal message for herself: *"respect the hands of my priests, they are the anointed ones"* Miryana has often expressed her irritation of priests, especially some of the questions they ask her. I have had trouble with priests but I will always respect the appointed office if not the man.

We walked home in silence, then shared our thoughts and experiences. Patrick had trembled quite violently during the apparition but as he looked at the sun he saw a golden monstrance, then a red heart and a baby. We had been reflecting on the words 'fruit of your womb'.

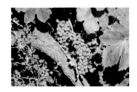

A Pilgrim's Diary

Easter 2007

The week before leaving for Medjugorje we had been "told" to pray the Divine Mercy Chaplet which begins on Good Friday and finishes on the Sunday after Easter.

To be honest, we had both resisted this prayer for several years, but in obedience, we agreed to pray it.

We arrived in Medjugorje on Tuesday night of Holy Week having nearly missed the train from St Pancras to Gatwick, and then arriving in Dubrovnik bus station at 5.20pm just in time for the last bus of the day which should have left at 5 00pm!.
I said a silent thank you prayer to my Guardian Angel Peter as we got on the bus.

We were warmly welcomed by Shane and Darren, our hosts, had pizza in Tomatos restaurant and a lot of laughter because I thought Patrick said he had made a promise to 'our Eddy'

"Who's 'our Eddy?' I asked. He had actually said 'Our Lady' …

Holy Wednesday.
Mass celebrated by a very slow-speaking Philipino priest. We climbed Podboro, praying the joyful and sorrowful mysteries en-route and went to confession. I was given good advice; to spend an hour a week before the Blessed Sacrament to 'feed our ministry', to have monthly confession no matter how 'small' the sin because it is humbling to get down on our knees before our God, to always praise and give thanks to God, to remember that whether separated, divorced, married or single, the most important relationship we have is with God.

Holy Thursday.
It was cold and wet, so we went to a book shop. I always ask the Lord what He wants me to read and I picked up Sr Faustina's diary. (She had the vision of the Divine Mercy of Jesus) We prayed all day and went to the church early for the Mass of the Last Supper but couldn't get a seat so we stood for two hours. A power cut this evening so no hot food or heat - a real pilgrimage!

Good Friday.
The day started with us being asked to share in an experience of the Scourging, the Thirst and the Crucifixion of Jesus. I stood at the foot of the Cross with Mary and the other women, while Patrick shared in the above.
Then we climbed Krusevec. We carried up with us all those for whom we had been asked to pray.
As we climbed we were overtaken by seven men in their twenties singing a hymn in their native tongue.
I was rooted to the spot and transported back in time.

To me it was the disciple John leading the other disciples on the very first pilgrimage up Calvary.

Good Friday.
I imagined John telling the others who had run away – "this is where He fell, this is where He met his mother, this is where they pulled a man out of the crowd to help Him carry the Cross, this is where a woman ran up to meet Him to wipe His face and he left an impression of His face on her cloth, this is where He spoke to the women "…..

Imagine after the Resurrection and Ascension, how John would be bold enough to go up Calvary again and recount that awful journey.

We left a letter and a photo with Mary at the foot of the cross on Krusevec – given us in Derby. We gave Jesus all those we have prayed for, and our families and our ministry.
On the way down the seven young men passed us again – still singing – Patrick started to sing "There's a Cross for everyone to bear" and a couple thanked him and asked where he was from. The man was from Cork and they now live in Andorra. We chatted about ourselves and I had a feeling we would be seeing them again.
At 3 00pm we went to the English service in St James' Church. Our Lady's statue has a white veil over it as if she is in mourning until Her son arises.

As we left the church the Cork couple ran after us and asked us to pray with a woman called Anya. She is Irish and had married a local man and is now a guide in Medjugorje.
She has four children and asked for prayer for her eight year old daughter, Natalie, who has something like autism and is not able to speak. Patrick placed his hand on her throat and prayed in proxy through her.
He shook as the Holy Spirit took hold.
Anja was going to the holy Land on Easter Sunday where her son was making his first Holy Communion so we would not see her again. We went home and continued to pray for Natalie.
We began the Chaplet of Divine Mercy.

Holy Saturday.
We spent all day in prayer in preparation. At 3pm we listened to the seven scripture readings in English, then at 8pm the locals attended their Vigil Mass in St James' Church which was broadcast in the packed yellow hall.

Communion was brought over to us in the pouring rain. Crowds of people who could not get inside the church stood outside for two hours under umbrellas, privileged to be there.

Later we returned to St James' Church for an hour long vigil. The church was packed and so we stood or knelt for the very special hour of graced silence, prayer and music.

At midnight there was incredible Joy and spontaneous applause.

Easter Sunday.
Thank God! We spent the morning sharing on how it might have been on that first Easter Day for Mary, the other women and disciples, the locals and the guards.

English mass was at midday and full of Joy.

The Mass was celebrated by a priest from Vietnam. He told us that four hundred people were being baptised in his parish church this Easter. There was no problem with him being in Medjugorje for Easter because they had more than sufficient priests in his diocese.

Fr Kevin Devine, a priest from New York who now lives in Medjugorje to serve the English speaking pilgrims, was also on the altar. (We call him Homer because he sounds just like Homer in the Simpsons) He was overwhelmed with the news about the baptisms because as a young priest he was an army chaplain serving in Vietnam. He recalled driving in a jeep with a French bishop who used to say "They want to kill me because I'm a missionary and they want to kill you because you're an American."

'Homer' was delighted to be con-celebrating Mass with a priest from the area that he had been serving and trying to liberate.

In the evening we celebrated with a wonderful meal in Dubrovnik restaurant – the best meal ever in Medjugorje! – or did it just taste better after the Lenten fast?

Easter Monday.

We checked our emails in the morning. I had email requests from our diocese and family and on our ministry website there was a request from a woman asking for prayers for her son who had told her he often heard demonic voices in his head.

As Patrick read this he was thrown back as if jabbed in the stomach. We prayed for protection and for the young man and his family, and overcame it.

Patrick eventually managed to send a reply to her to tell her we were praying. Darren and Shane, our hosts, witnessed this so we went for a coffee for a chat and then took all requests to Mass at noon.

During the Mass the priest invoked the Peace of Jesus and passed it on.

I was surrounded with a beautiful scent of Peace.

We were at the back of church next to an elderly woman who was sitting on a fold-up stool.

Patrick was told by Our Lady *"tell her how much my Son loves her"*
So after Communion (he had to nudge the priest to give her Communion because she could not stand up to join the queue) he told her this and gave her a white Rosary beads he had bought the previous day (for someone but didn't know who) and her eyes filled with tears.

As we received Jesus, Patrick shook and she held onto his hand.

A very special Mass.

We walked to Podboro in the afternoon and bought some lavender and cloths to wipe on the weeping Risen Lord statue.

Easter Monday.

We wanted to go to the evening Mass and Healing prayers but we couldn't get into church because it was so full.

People were crammed in and standing outside under umbrellas in the rain and hail.

The next morning Patrick told me he couldn't sleep during the night because he had been very agitated by his clothes, his quilt cover and a nauseating smell which filled his head, his room and the whole apartment.

Easter Monday.

He thought it came from the perfumed cloths we had been given by the " lavender" woman. He got up and went out for a walk in the pouring rain, disposing of the cloths in a bin, then he walked some more and prayed. When he returned he showered, and was then able to sleep. I hadn't noticed anything unusual during the night.

I understood this was an attack – imitating the scent associated with Our Lady so we prayed for protection and went to Mass.

Easter Tuesday.

A lot more pilgrims have arrived, including a big group from America. Their priests seem to be particularly large – one of them on the altar sits looking like buddha.

An Irish priest spoke of Mary's frequent apparitions and likened them to an anxious mother whose child is in intensive care –

hence her desire to visit often and watch over this world which is in intensive care.

We were very mindful of a woman having a mastectomy today in Canada. We prayed for her at the Blue Cross. Patrick was quite ill – and was actually sick on return home.

Then three hours in church for Rosary, Mass and Healing Prayers.

Ate cake, drank coke and back for an hour of Adoration. Mighty powerful. As we stood waiting in a packed church my heart leapt as the priest placed the Host in the monstrance.

It was as if Jesus had come over the hill and stood on the mount before us.

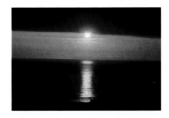

"Do not be afraid, I love you. I have carved you in the palm of my hand. I will be with you for all time" rang in my head.

Easter Wednesday.

Woke to sunshine after days of rain, hail, cold and power cuts!

What a homily! Probably the best one in twenty two years of visiting Medjugorje, given by a man from the west coast of Ireland who spoke very fast and with a great sense of humour.

The gospel was the Road to Emmaus.

Jesus took the bread, blessed it, broke it, shared it.

He takes us (at our birth) blesses us (at our baptism) but not until He breaks us are we ready to be used by Him.

Only in our brokenness can we be of any good to others.

The priest had carried a cross since an incident in his childhood. As he walked with a friend from Jerusalem to Emmaus he carried a rosary which he thought would be a treasure for life and was disappointed on reaching Emmaus to find that the Crucifix had fallen off his rosary. His friend suggested it was a grace – that he no longer carried this cross.

He reminded us of the visionary Vicka who had terrible head pain. Our Lady offered to relieve it but Vicka said she would keep it and offers it up for the souls in Purgatory.

Mary gives us five methods of prayer:

Two are for our Purification – Fasting and Penance,
Three are to Feed us – The Rosary, Scripture and Holy Mass.

As we shared the Peace of Christ he told us that the twin of peace is joy and to "wrap your peace up with a smile"

Medjugorje is not a place but a spirituality. Some say "why can't it be like this at home?" but it can be if we take it back with us. We take the spirituality home with us and others want to know where we get our joy from.

If we bring just one person to Medjugorje we are passing on our love and joy.

Christmas may be for women but Easter appeals more to the men – blood and guts and betrayal.

It is said that a man needs a good woman but who better than Our Lady?

Easter Wednesday.

A man went to the doctor and saw small arrows painted on the wall just above the skirting board.

He followed them till he came to a notice on the wall. He knelt down to read it and it said - you are now in the correct position to receive your injection.

In the same way we in Medjugorje are in the correct position to receive our injection from Mary.

He broke the bread at Consecration and said:

"Partake of this bread to feed your life"

and at the words of dismissal:

"This Mass is ended, now go and continue with the Mass of your life"

We left feeling well fed and nourished with the Word and Eucharist.

Reading the above I realise there is nothing new here but we have been here a week now, have been to confession, fasted and done penance and are receptive to receive…

The miracle of Medjugorje has taken place.

We walked to Krusevec through the vines.

They are bare now and hang together in the shape of crosses, all well pruned and stark.

We realise that when Jesus broke the bread for the two disciples on the road to Emmaus it was not the Last Supper they recognised but the Crucifixion.

We remembered a previous visit when we met a Dublin man on Mt Krusevec.

He asked us to explain a dream he had in which he was carrying something very precious in the palm of his hand. He "knew" he would meet someone on the mountain who would explain it!

We told him it was the Host and he was to explain the Real Presence to people.

We now recognise this as a foretaste to our ministry – explaining the Real Presence and connection to Calvary and our Passion experiences.

Easter Wednesday.

"I am broken for you so you may eat and live"

"For you I descended from Heaven to earth. For you I allowed Myself to be nailed to the Cross.

For you I let my Sacred Heart be pierced with a lance, opening wide the Source of Mercy for you.

Come with trust to draw graces from this fountain. I never reject a contrite heart.

Your misery has disappeared in the depths of My mercy.

Do not argue with Me about your wretchedness.

You will please Me and do My Will if you hand over to Me all your troubles and griefs.

I will heap upon you the Treasures of My grace"

This is Christ speaking through us of His Forgiveness and Love. He is the source for all healing.

Easter Thursday.

Mass celebrated by an Irish bishop, Brendan. We had met him last year when he introduced himself as "My name is Brendan and I am an alcoholic All of us need to face the truth about ourselves and be freed from denial through the Grace of God"
"God is not mad at you - He is mad about you."

He told us to take home the sure knowledge that God loves us and that was why He created us.

Easter Thursday.

He spoke of the tendency for men to come up to him and say "I'm not very religious but…" or

"I'm not a good Catholic but…"

This annoyed him for years until he was given the response.

"So I hear"

They would object "What do you mean! Who told you?" and he would reply "Well, you just did!"

Leonard Cohen, a poet and songwriter, wrote a poem about a dialogue between his soul and God. God said:

"You have loved a lot, now will you let me love you?"

So many of us have been busy doing and giving and loving.

God says *"Would you ever be still and let me love you?"*

After Mass we were entertained by a young Irish crowd singing and dancing outside. The bishop had inspired them and filled them with joy – the youth of the church.

Later we met the elderly woman whom Patrick had prayed with in church and been given a message for. She and her daughter were

delighted because they had carried a gift around with them for two days hoping to bump into him.

She had bought a Divine Mercy rosary and a miraculous medal. Her name was Celine so we nicknamed her Dion and she was from Tralee – Patrick's place of birth. She was Glowing full of Joy.

In the evening we took part in the Rosary, Mass and Adoration. We were praying for a young friend aged twelve who has a tumour on his brain.

During the Mass we happened to sit behind a boy of about the same age.

At the time of consecration a side door opened to reveal a golden sun with a white Host in front of it.

The sun was spinning and it caused Patrick to shake as the Holy Spirit took hold of him.

The boy in front was fascinated – looking at the sun and then at Patrick.

Easter Thursday.

When we were invited to share a sign of peace the boy enthusiastically turned round with a big smile and a firm hand shake. We 'took' our young friend Matthew, in spirit to receive Communion with us and when we returned to our seat I noticed the boy in front had a nose bleed which was quickly dealt with by his Gran.

It seemed to affirm that our prayer for Matthew had been heard.

Easter Friday.

Mass was celebrated by a priest from Australia who told us of his beautiful homeland where his parishioners had wealth and wonderful houses but lacked love and compassion. He carried a great sadness and he really had no knowledge to impart or inspire us.

We went back for the evening services and got a seat in church by getting there an hour and half before they were due to start.

The rosary begins at 5 00pm before Mass an hour later.

There is a pause about 5.40pm for the time of daily apparition.

However it was a bit marred by a group of six Irish women sitting in front of us who literally pushed a man out of their pew so the six of them could sit together!. Patrick was not impressed!

Easter Saturday.

An early walk at dawn was rewarded by meeting a group of Irish teenagers on their way to climb Krusevec. "Isn't it great to be able to do it!" they said. What a wonderful contrast to the example shown by their elders the previous evening at Mass The old ways and attitudes need to make way for this new love of life and neighbour.

This was our last day so we went to confession to receive the strengthening grace of the Sacrament before returning home.

There were long queues everywhere but one door was open and no-one seemed to be going in so Patrick went inside.

He was surprised to find 'buddha' sitting there, and even more surprised to find he shared very similar mystical experiences and they had a great chat. 'Buddha' turned out to be a Fr Peter from

Easter Saturday.

America who asked if he could share what he had heard with 'the folks back home' and asked Patrick for his penance to pray for all those in Medjugorje who were not well and for all abortions.

He also encouraged the Divine Mercy prayer and St Louis de Montfort's consecration to Our Lady.

I also went to him for confession. The first time I have been greeted in confession with the word "Wow!" – Fr Peter was recovering from the Patrick experience and had seen Patrick and I exchange a few words as I was going in!

Patrick was not well after confession and it took me a while to realise this was because of the penance he had been given – to pray for all in Medjugorje who were not well and had come for healing and pray for girls/women who had abortions – he was now carrying their grief and pain.

We went home. Darren had seen us and was concerned because Patrick looked so ill.

He knocked on his door to ask if he was alright and then asked for prayer for himself and was with us for three hours during which he received a lot of peace, love and forgiveness.

Final Day.

The next morning we went to get a bus back to Dubrovnik.

We were joined by a woman from Dublin, and there were only three of us on the bus.

She was a lovely woman who gave me details of a house to bring a group next year.

She told us about herself and listened to our stories.

I had a feeling she was sent to accompany us on our journey home because she reminded us to do certain things on our return, and seemed to know us really well.

Her name was Mary.

When we told her that we prayed through the intercession of Padre Pio and Our Lady she pointed to the windscreen of the bus where there was a picture of Padre Pio. Patrick immediately shook when he saw it. I had a feeling we would be going to San Giovanni soon.

Final Day.

Indeed, we visited San Giovanni a few months later and went straight to the church where his body was in repose. We arrived just before 3pm on a Friday and there was a long queue of people with tickets to file past his body in veneration. Somehow we just walked in and I suggested we sit in a raised area used for liturgies which overlooked Padre's body. At 2.55 a steward came to usher us all out but when I turned to tell Patrick we had to leave it was too late – he had already begun to share a mystical passion and crucifixion. I prayed to the Lord "If you want us to stay here You had better make us invisible!" And it seems He did because everyone else left apart from a nun and ourselves. While Patrick shared with Jesus, I prayed for our families and all who had asked us for prayer. Later that evening Patrick slipped on some stairs and hurt himself badly - jolting his shoulders, hip and knee as well as cutting his elbow and head. I suggested we visited the hospital but he would not go and asked me to help him to his room. ...... I cleaned his head and bandaged his elbow and left him to rest. I asked Padre Pio to come and pray for him while he slept. Patrick had an eventful night - he had a dream in which Padre Pio visited him, put his hand on his head, blessed him and healed him. When he woke there was no sign of a damaged back, hip or knee, and his elbow and head had both completely healed, no cuts or bruises anywhere, and we were able to go for a long walk.

On the last night of our pilgrimage I was having trouble sleeping so I thought I would pray for single mums who were feeling lonely and desperate and then I fell asleep and dreamt that I was with the young Mary being woken in the middle of the night by Joseph and being told he had dreamt that they had got to leave immediately for Egypt. I helped her gather her belongings and carried the baby when she needed a rest. It was as if I was her mother. I was very aware of my own grandmother being very close to me – she seemed to be just a few feet above me.

The next morning I told Patrick I had been on a journey to Egypt !

Home Again.

On our return home to Derby we were delighted to open an email from the mother of the satanist who said he had cut his long hair, got rid of satanic music, felt he had been living in a fog for three years.

Those who knew him couldn't believe the changes in him.

He was literally the talk of the parish and beyond!

He had been to Mass and received Holy Communion with her on Easter Sunday.

His father and sister also went to mass, as did some long lost cousins. The family now have a monthly gathering to say the rosary.

Praise Jesus!

The first answer phone message I listened to was from a woman we had visited in hospital with cancer who said "From the moment you left the ward I began to recover and I feel great.

I have been discharged and my family can't believe the difference in me. I am filled with Peace." Thank you God !

We had also prayed for a friend of the young satinist who had many problems and were delighted to receive a phone call from his mother the afternoon we got back saying he was healed and back at Mass!

Perhaps an even greater wonder (but then again maybe not) is that both of these teenage boys went to Medjugorje together some months later.

Their Mums went with them to the airport, tears of gratitude and joy as they saw the plane take off.

In Medjugorje the lads were very embarrassed at all the attention they received from mums asking them for the "secret" and how could they get their sons to go to Mass never mind Medjugorje!

We are so Blessed in our Ministry of Prayer and Healing.

Come Holy Spirit

Medjugorje/Walsingham May 2009

Consecration to Our Lady

Just as I resisted the Divine Mercy chaplet for three years, so I resisted St Louis de Montford's recommendation of a 33 day consecration to Our Lady. But the time comes when we have to humbly bow down and acknowledge we are nothing but servants and so on Good Friday I began the Divine Mercy chaplet and the Prayers of Consecration which was timed to end on the feast day of Our Lady of Fatima, May 13th.

In December, Patrick had booked 2 days in Walsingham for this feast day but at the time I had no idea I would be concluding the 33 days of prayer to consecrate myself to Our Lady.

During this time of consecration we spent a week in Medjugorje which was probably the most personal and prayerful pilgrimage yet – also the most simple.

We stayed at the house of Ivan and Janya, about 25 minutes walk from the church so walked a lot. On the 2nd of May we went to the Blue Cross to be present for Miryana's apparition and climbed above it, so we were looking down on the thousands who had gathered on the hillside. During the apparition, Patrick shook with spiritual energy and as it ended I watched about twelve swallows accompany Mary as she left. They circled round and round and upwards in a spiral until out of sight – then the silence broke and we all returned to normal. Miryana's words were interpreted into many languages. She said Our Lady was sad today.

This feeling of sadness stayed with me all day until I went to the sacrament of reconciliation to a Polish priest who reminded me that Our Lady calls herself the Queen of Peace, and Jesus' first words after His resurrection were *"I give you peace"* I was told to hold onto that peace and let nothing disturb me. It did the trick! I was sad for family and friends who reject Jesus, who try to do things alone rather than turn to Him, who do not read the signs of the times.

Medjugorje/Walsingham May 2009

Bishop Brendan happened to be there on the Monday and told a story of a three year old whose mummy had died. The child asked him "Is there a kitchen in the house of God?" Brendan told us that there certainly is a kitchen, and the men standing behind him on the altar wearing white garments were the waiters and were going to serve us the banquet of a lifetime! God made us because He loves us, He wants to serve us and for us to be happy. So simple and yet we have complicated it.

On the Tuesday, an English priest told us how he had asked Our Lady to teach him how to love Jesus like she does. During the Mass he totally forgot the words of consecration. His mind went blank – then his head was filled with the words "This is My Son" Wow!!

The most important truth I learnt from this pilgrimage was the need to save our own soul first, then help others to save theirs through prayer, humility, obedience and joy.

The most important relationship we have is our relationship with God. If that is good then all others fall into place.

A week after Medjugorje we went to Walsingham for a couple of days. It was beautiful – an English gem. The Catholic shrine is traditional, full of history and stones of courage and fortitude . The Anglican shrine is magnificent and on the feast day of Our Lady of Fatima we went to a ceremony in the Anglican shrine called the 'Sprinkling of Water' After a short talk on the history of the spring we were invited to go down some steps to the spring water where the priest gave each person a mouthful of water on a ladle. As I supped the water off the ladle (or rather he poured it into my mouth) I felt it's purity rush through me. I am sure I have never tasted water so good – it filled me like a living spring – cleansing, empowering, refreshing. He then ladled water over my hands (which held a rosary which had turned gold!) saying the words

"Through the power of God the Father, be healed at the intercession of Our Lady of Walsingham"

.... I have always felt I'm a bit of a pet of Our Lady but now I feel well and truly adopted!

HOMILIES

Homilies.

"If you do not go home changed, you have missed the point!"

After many years of visiting Medjugorje it is amazing how I find the homilies boring/ old-fashioned or uninspiring at the beginning of a pilgrimage, but towards the end I think they are all wonderful!

It took me a while to work out that rather than the quality of the preacher, it was ME that had changed!

These homilies are offered to help you change as these priests have opened themselves to the Holy Spirit, to Mary's guidance, and most of all to God's love.

Vocations through Mary.

Fr Jim a priest from Dublin who has been ordained less than a year. He entered the seminary aged forty three following years of drugs, promiscuity and materialism.

He was an engineer working in California when his younger sister bought him a ticket to Medjugorje.

He did not want to go but decided not to offend his sister. He had always sought an elusive peace, trying to find it in the world but here, in Medjugorje, he found Christ's peace which entered his heart for the first time. He came to Medjugorje again and soon decided he was called to be a priest.

Fr Ed a priest now working in America but originally from Cork. He came to Medjugorje 17 years ago as a single man, out of curiosity, and as he climbed Krusevec he asked Our Lady for direction.

He was asked "When are you going to act?" he discussed it with a Franciscan priest who said "You Irish are all the same, you can't make up your mind; that's why you get married so late!"

He was told to look into his heart and read what the fax from Our Lady said to him.

Vocations through Mary.

He considered his options and thought he could get married, have a family, wash the car at weekends and have a dog!

Instead, he went home and joined a seminary in September but six months later he walked out because he wasn't coping with the academics.

He returned to Medjugorje in March, a broken man. He spoke to the Franciscans, climbed Krusevec, consecrated himself to Our Lady, and vowed to return to the seminary and never walk away again. With great humility he returned to the seminary with his two cases as his friends jibed him:

"How long are you going to stay this time?"

After a while he was thrown out because he couldn't pass his exams – but he remembered his vow and went to another seminary.

This one, in Mississippi, was dedicated to Our Lady, and was different again. The seminarians prayed the rosary around her statue at 10pm every night. He came back to Medjugorje for his pre-ordination retreat.

When he returned to be ordained he was told by his pastor that a fax had arrived from the nuns in Medjugorje -

"Congratulations Ed on your ordination"

He knew this was confirmation from Our Lady herself. He offered this Mass for all priests – that we would all have a better understanding of vocation.

Perseverance.

Fr Bill a Spirit-filled priest from Nova Scotia. He had been brought up in a catholic family and his teenage years were focused on sport and being popular.

When he was fifteen he was diagnosed with lupus which meant he couldn't go out into the sun without total covering. Medication controlled the lupus and he went to college when he was eighteen but after a year the lupus flared up again and he had to return home.

At college though he had met a Pentecostal lad who had told him how he could have a personal relationship with Jesus and told him to read the gospels. When he returned home and was quite ill he felt it was worth 'giving Jesus a go'.

He read the gospels, went to a Pentecostal church and became a Christian. He worked hard, was prominent in his church but began to consider his catholic roots again. He studied the catholic catechism alongside scripture and found they were compatible! He returned to the catholic church and went to a catholic theology college for a year, and thought he might meet a nice catholic girl and marry.

He returned to Halifax to work and incredibly walked away from the catholic church again for twenty years. When he returned to his home town he joined a prayer group and a woman asked him if he had ever thought about being a priest. He had not considered it, but it felt so right so he went to see his bishop. This was his first time in Medjugorje. He spoke of the wonder of free expression here in prayer – some with arms outstretched, some on their knees and bowed down, and some praying before Our Lady's statue.

When he was in the prayer group he was asked

"What role has Mary played in your life?"

He pondered before replying "I guess she has always been interceding for me" He spoke of our crosses and the need to surrender our lives to Jesus; how Jesus has a plan for each of us but we must not invent our own crosses. When we surrender our lives to Jesus' plan we find the crosses He asks us to carry are lighter and manageable because He helps us. When we choose to carry crosses of our own making they are heavy and burdensome because they come with guilt and burdens.

Forgiveness and Healing.

Fr Pat a priest from Cork, now working in Leeds, told us of a time he was visiting a hospital and was given the wrong bed number.

"Are you Mr Shaw?"

"No"

"Are you a Catholic?"

"I used to be"

"Do you want to talk or shall I go away?"

"Sit down"

This man's mother had died when he was ten years of age, his wife died when she was twenty four after one year of marriage.

When the priest asked him if he prayed the man asked "Who or what to?" the priest advised him to say "If there's anyone there please help!" He visited him for the next three years and then there was a knock at the priest's door and the man's brother was asking him to visit urgently.

The man was dying and asked for the Sacraments. He received Reconciliation, the Eucharist and Anointing of the sick. He lived for three more days, squeezed the priest's hand and said "I'm so happy"

He used the analogy of Krusevec as a symbol of our life.

From the distance we can see the Cross on the summit. We set out on our journey called Life. As we climb we can no longer see the Cross, at times we can only see the rocks ahead and we lose sight of the goal.

Forgiveness and Healing.

Fr Ed from Boston, celebrated Mass and told us that he first came to Medjugorje in 1984 knowing nothing about the place, but he saw it as a free trip to Europe. He was struck by the simple faith and truth of the six children.

He met Manuko, the man who gave the two girls a lift in his car on the morning of June 25th, 1981. They told him they had seen Gospa on the hill the night before and he went cold with fright.

He believed them though, even when Fr Joso did not, and protected them from the police and soldiers. He was arrested as a ring leader and accused of planning a hoax but the children went to the police station and said he was innocent –

"Release him and take us instead" Their courage had a big effect on Fr Ed and the word he took home from Medjugorje was:

"Tell the others"

When he returned to Boston he met a wealthy business man who wanted to spread the message of Medjugorje and asked Fr Ed how to do so. Fr Ed suggested a video and came back with him while he did the filming. This was later translated into fifteen languages and helped to pass Our Lady's message throughout the world.

Fr Ed shared that he thought he would become holy once he was a priest but as the years passed by he was only more aware of his own sinfulness. He knew that the hardest thing for people to accept was God's love for them yet they took no convincing of their own sin.

He failed to apply this to himself.

One evening at a prayer group he felt his own sinfulness was consuming him and he was enveloped in a chronic back pain, so severe that an ambulance had to be called. He could not lie in the ambulance but had to kneel on one knee. In hospital the pain worsened – he still had to kneel and morphine failed to ease his pain.

He was diagnosed with having kidney stones.

Forgiveness and Healing.

A priest friend, Fr Jim, came to visit him and Ed told him to find a bible.

He returned with a bible saying "I could only find a Gideon's!" Ed told him to read it and Jim said "What shall I read?" "Anything" said Ed so Jim opened it at random and read Job "All the years that have been eaten away by the locusts will be replenished"

Ed knew that the kidney stones represented the sins that had to be forgiven and cleansed.

He spoke of Spiritual Truth – unlike material truth – the more you give away the more you receive. We have to give away what we have received from God, and we thus receive more.

I have been healed and therefore I have to pass it on to others. I feel this with great conviction.

Ed blessed us 'In the name of the father, in the blood of the Son, in the power of the Holy Spirit'

Mercy and Forgiveness.

Fr John sang of Mercy and prayed for us to forgive all those who had hurt us.

He spoke of those with special needs and the blessings they bring. His own uncle had special needs and for a while lived with three single alcoholic brothers.

One night one of them stabbed him with a hypodermic needle used to inject heroin.

He became ill and walked three kilometres to his sister's house. She bathed him because he stank so much and she noticed the mark of the needle because it had become infected, so she took him to hospital where he was nursed back to health.

If she had not taken him he could well have died.

This man was called Mark and he was once outside with his nephew and told him to look up at the tree, and asked him what he saw.

The boy replied "A leaf?" and Mark replied "That's God"

Mercy and Forgiveness.

A bird was singing sweetly and he asked the boy "What do you hear?" the boy (a quick learner!) replied "God?" Mark smiled broadly and said "Yes….God is everywhere"

The simplicity of faith had a great impact on the boy who grew up to have a vocation to the priesthood with a particular compassion to those with special needs. He then asked us all to close our eyes and he sang a song of Mercy. We were all anointed with God's love and mercy. We must forgive as we are forgiven.

Fr Peter began with one of my favourite stories about the three year old asking to be alone with her baby brother. Her parents hesitated at first but her insistence won them over.

They listened on the intercom when she entered her little brother's bedroom; she crept up to the cot and said:
"Tell me about God because I'm beginning to forget!" We have a conscious recollection of God until we are about thirty months old and then it fades. Before our soul leaves God, he kisses us tenderly and appoints our guardian angel and our soul departs His kingdom and enters our body at the point of conception.

Sacrament of Reconciliation. God's Love For Us.

Bishop Brendan from Wexford stood up and said "I'm Brendan and I'm an alcoholic!"
Such honesty then poured from him which filled us all with grace. He spoke with passion of God's love – the love of God the father as described in the parable of the prodigal son.
The father who runs to meet his son. What if this son had returned and the farm was locked up and there was a sign saying 'gone Fishing'?

Sacrament of Reconciliation. God's Love For Us.

Between the Ascension and the descent of the Holy Spirit, Mary was the constancy. She would not leave the upper room until He returned. Peter, rather than a rock was a trampoline and said "I'm going fishing", and others followed him. God is raving mad about us, distracted entirely – especially for sinners.

Then Bishop Brendan spoke of the sacrament of reconciliation and the miracle of Medjugorje when you look at the queues for confession.

When people say 'I'd rather speak directly to God', reply 'Tell Jesus that – He needn't have bothered dying for the forgiveness of your sins!'

Think of the joy you feel after you receive the sacrament – you never

feel that good after talking to God directly!

Then he addressed the twenty priests behind him –
why do less people partake of the sacrament?" "Because priests don't regularly receive the sacrament themselves.

If priests practised it regularly then they could preach about it. How can you preach of it's beauty unless you live it? How important is it to be in the church with the door open on a regular basis.

You may sit there for a few weeks in prayer and no-one comes; then someone may come because they feel sorry for you – but will receive such tender grace that they will tell others and more will come.

Much better than having a sign saying 'Gone Fishing' "

Remember two things – Surrender and Fidelity – here in Medjugorje we surrender our lives to God – give Him everything.

Then He gives it back to us in chunks as we can handle it,

<u>and we must be faithful to Him in the little things.</u>

Go in Peace.

Forgiveness

If we accept that death is part of life
And that we die a little every day
Then we will not postpone
The showing of affection
The kindly deed
The loving word
But we will do it now
Because the time is now
If we forgive as we
Would be forgiven
And do it now
Before it is too late
We will have no regrets
When and loved ones, friends and others die
And go their silent way
We will not fret
Or have that nagging doubt
About
What might have been
If only …
What might have been
What could have been
What should have been
Too late!
The time is Now
To do what we would do
If we but knew
Today was the last day
The listening ear could hear
 The Words We Meant To Say
The Time Is Now

Patrick Lynch & Alison Riggott.